A New Text of the Apocalypse from Spain: Extracted and Translated from the Latin Text of the Morgan Ms. of the Eighth Century Commentary of the Spanish Presbyter, Beatus

Beatus, Edgar Simmons Buchanan

Copyright © BiblioLife, LLC

This historical reproduction is part of a unique project that provides opportunities for readers, educators and researchers by bringing hard-to-find original publications back into print at reasonable prices. Because this and other works are culturally important, we have made them available as part of our commitment to protecting, preserving and promoting the world's literature. These books are in the "public domain" and were digitized and made available in cooperation with libraries, archives, and open source initiatives around the world dedicated to this important mission.

We believe that when we undertake the difficult task of re-creating these works as attractive, readable and affordable books, we further the goal of sharing these works with a global audience, and preserving a vanishing wealth of human knowledge.

Many historical books were originally published in small fonts, which can make them very difficult to read. Accordingly, in order to improve the reading experience of these books, we have created "enlarged print" versions of our books. Because of font size variation in the original books, some of these may not technically qualify as "large print" books, as that term is generally defined; however, we believe these versions provide an overall improved reading experience for many.

A NEW TEXT

OF

THE APOCALYPSE

FROM SPAIN

Extracted and Translated from the Latin Text of
THE MORGAN MS. OF THE EIGHTH CENTURY
COMMENTARY OF THE SPANISH PRESBYTER

BEATUS

BY

E. S. BUCHANAN, M. A., B. Sc.

(Lecturer in the year 1915 on
Classical Philology, University of Michigan)

Editor of Oxford Old-Latin Biblical Texts: Nos. V and VI;
Sacred Latin Texts: Nos. I, II and III;
The Records Unrolled;
The Irish (Latin) Gospels in English;
The Search for the Original Words of the Gospel;
Etc., Etc.

NEW YORK
1915

Copies of this *New Text of the Apocalypse from Spain* may be obtained from the Paget Literary Agency, 25 W. 45th St., New York. Price, 50 cents post paid. Remittance to be sent with order.

By the same writer.

The Search for the Original Words of the Gospel: A lecture delivered at Union Theological Seminary, New York, 1914. Copies are still obtainable from the Paget Literary Agency. Price, 25 cents post paid.

Foreword

On October 20th, 1914, I was shewn in the Library of Mr. J. P. Morgan of New York a Latin MS. of the Commentary of the Spanish presbyter Beatus on the Apocalypse. The vigor of the tenth century paintings in the MS. was surprising, but equally surprising was the MS.'s Biblical text. Where it departed from the Vulgate, the Latin vocabulary was African, and agreed with that employed by Cyprian and Primasius. There was also a surprising agreement with the only verse of the Apocalypse quoted in that most ancient of Irish MSS.—the Antiphonary of Bangor, now at Milan. The Bangor Book's single verse (Apoc. vii. 14) gives us three new readings; and all these three new readings are now found in the text of our MS.

For four months I occupied myself in New York in transcribing from the Commentary the text of the Apocalypse, and was then allowed by its owner to study the MS. with greater facilities in the Library of the University of Michigan. Since March 16th the MS. has been at Ann Arbor, and has engaged all my time and attention.

At the request of some friends I have prepared the English translation that follows, to shew to the reader unacquainted with Latin the new light thrown on the darkest book in the Bible by the recovery of the ancient Spanish, or Irish, or African form of its text. It will be seen that this form is very considerably different from that found in the American Standard Edition, which is based on the unhappy English Revised Version of 1881.

We are still at some distance from the recovery of the actual first form of the New Testament writings; but every new text helps forward our knowledge, dissipates our ignorance and loosens the fetters of finality and dogmatism which have so sadly impeded the progress of the truth in past generations. The MS. was copied (as we learn from the Scribe himself) at Tabara in Spain in 968-970 A. D. The date of its copying does not detract from the fact that it embodies in the main a second century text tradition, than which we have at present no earlier.

In the Name of Our Lord Jesus Christ
Beginneth
The Revelation
of
Our Lord Jesus Christ

BOOK THE FIRST

1 The Revelation of Jesus Christ, which God gave unto him, to shew unto his servants things which must shortly come to pass; and he sent and signified *it* by his messenger unto his servant John:

2 Who bare witness to the Word of God.

3 Blessed *is* he that readeth, and he that heareth the words of prophecy, and keepeth those things which are written therein: for the time *is* at hand.

4 John to the seven churches: Grace is yours, and peace, from God which is, and which was, and which is to come;

5 Even from Jesus Christ, *who is* the faithful witness, *and* the firstbegotten of the dead, and the prince of the kings of the earth. He that loved us hath also washed us from our sins in blood,

6 And hath made us a kingdom of priests unto God and his Father. Glory is his for ever and ever.

7 Behold, he shall come in the clouds; and every eye shall see him, and they *also* which pierced him: and all the kindreds of earth and of heaven shall see him such. Amen.

8 I am Alpha and Omega, the beginning and the

1. 8-20

ending, saith the Lord, which is, and which was, and which is to come, the Almighty.

9 I, John, your brother and companion in the tribulation and kingdom and patience of Jesus, was in the isle that is called Patmos, for the Word of God.

10 And I heard behind me a loud voice, like a trumpet,

11 Saying unto me, What things thou seest, write in a book, and take back to Ephesus, and Smyrna, and Pergamos, and Thyatira, and Sardis, and Philadelphia, and Laodicea.

12 And I turned and saw seven golden candlesticks;

13 And in the midst of the golden candlesticks *one* like unto the Son of man, clothed with a garment down to the foot, and girt about the paps with a golden girdle.

14 His head and *his* hair *were* white like white wool, or like snow; his eyes as a flame of fire;

15 And his feet like unto brass of Lebanon, as in a hot furnace; and his voice as the sound of many waters.

16 And he had in his right hand seven stars: and from his mouth a sharp twoedged sword proceeding. And his countenance *was* as when the sun shineth in its strength.

17 And when I saw him, I fell before his feet as dead. He laid his right hand upon me, saying, Fear not; I am the first and I am the last:

18 And the life; yet I died; and, behold, I am alive for evermore, Amen; and have the keys of death and of Hades.

19 Write therefore the things which thou hast seen, and the things which are, and the things which must be hereafter.

20 *Write* the meaning of the seven stars which thou sawest in my right hand, and of the seven candlesticks.

BOOK THE SECOND

Concerning the Seven Churches

1 For the messenger to the church of Ephesus write; These things saith he that holdeth the seven stars of the seven churches in his right hand, who walketh in the midst of the seven golden candlesticks;

2 I know thy works, and labour, and patience, and how thou canst not bear wicked men: and thou hast tried them which say they are apostles, and are not, and hast found them liars:

3 And *still* thou hast patience, and for my name's sake hast endured, and hast not fainted.

4 Nevertheless I have *somewhat* against thee, because thou hast left thy great love.

5 Remember from whence thou art fallen, and repent, and do the first works; or else I will come unto thee, and remove thy candlestick out of its place, unless thou hast repented.

6 But this good thing thou hast, that thou hatest the deeds of the Nicolaitans, which I also hate, saith the Lord.

7 He that hath an ear, let him hear what the Spirit saith unto the churches; To him that overcometh will I give to eat of the tree of life, which is in the paradise of my God.

8 For the messenger to the church of Smyrna write; These things saith the first and the last, which was dead, and is alive;

9 I know thy tribulation, and poverty, (but thou art rich); and *I know* thou art evil spoken of by them which say they are Jews, and are not, but *are* the synagogue of Satan.

10 Fear none of those things which thou shalt suffer: behold, the devil shall cast certain of you into

2. 10-20

prison, that ye may be tried; and ye shall have tribulation ten days: be thou faithful unto death, and I will give thee a crown of life.

11 He that hath ears, let him hear what the Spirit saith unto the churches, He that overcometh shall not be hurt by death.

12 For the messenger to the church of Pergamos write; These things saith he which hath the sharp sword with two edges;

13 I know where thou dwellest, *even* where Satan's seat *is:* and thou holdest fast my name, and didst not deny my faith in the days of Antipas, my faithful martyr, who was slain among you, where Satan dwelleth.

14 But I have a few things against thee, because thou hast there them that hold the teaching of Balaam, who taught Balak to cast a stumbling block before the children of Israel, that they might eat things sacrificed unto idols, and commit fornication.

15 So hast thou also those that hold the teaching of the Nicolaitans.

16 He that hath ears, let him hear what the Spirit saith unto the churches; To him that overcometh will I give to eat of the hidden manna. And I will give him a stone, and in the stone a new name written, which no one knoweth except him that receiveth *it.*

18 For the messenger to the church of Thyatira write; These things saith the Son of God, who hath eyes like a flame of fire, and feet like brass of Lebanon.

19 I know thy energy, and love, and faith, and service, and thy patience, and all thy works, the last even more abundant than the first.

20 I have much against thee, because thou sufferest that woman Jezebel, which calleth herself a prophetess

of God, to seduce many of my servants to commit fornication, and to eat things sacrificed unto idols.

21 And I gave her space to repent; and she would not repent of her fornication; and *still* teacheth and seduceth my servants to commit fornication.

22 Behold, I will cast her into a bed, and them that commit fornication with her into great tribulation, except they repent of her deeds:

23 And I will kill her children with death. In the end, all the churches shall know that I am he which searcheth hearts. and will give unto every one of you according to his works.

24 But unto you I say, that are left in Thyatira, I will put upon you no other burden.

25 Nevertheless that which ye have *already*, hold fast till I come.

26 And he that overcometh, and keepeth my works unto the end, to him will I give power over the nations:

27 And he shall rule them with an iron hand, and as a potter's vessel is broken, so shall they be broken in pieces.

1 For the messenger to the church of Sardis write; These things saith he that hath the seven stars; I know thy works, that thou hast a name that thou livest, and art dead.

2 Be watchful, and strengthen the things which remain, that are ready to die: for I have not found thy works upright before God.

3 Remember therefore how thou hast heard, and hast received the Holy Spirit, and repent. But if thou do not watch, I will come unto thee as a thief, and thy children know not what hour I will come upon thee.

4 But thou hast a few names in Sardis which have not defiled their garments; and they shall walk with me in white: for they are worthy.

3. 5-15

5 He that overcometh, so clothed in white raiment, I will not blot out his name out of the book of life, but I will confess his name before my Father, and before his angels.

6 He that hath ears, let him hear what the Spirit saith unto the churches.

7 For the messenger to the church of Philadelphia write; These things saith he that is holy, and true, he that hath the key of David, he that openeth, and no man shutteth; and shutteth, and no man openeth;

8 Behold, I have set before thee an open door. I know that thou hast *but* a little strength, and yet thou hast kept my word, and hast not denied my name.

9 Behold, certain of the synagogue of Satan, which say they are Jews, and are not, but do lie; behold, I will make them to come and worship before thy feet, and to know that I have loved thee.

10 Because thou hast kept the word of my patience, I also will keep thee from the hour of temptation, which shall come upon all the world, to try them that dwell upon the earth.

11 I will come quickly: hold thou fast that which thou hast, that another take not thy crown.

12 He that overcometh I will make him a pillar in the temple of my God, and he shall go no more out: and I will write upon him the name of my God, and the name of the new Jerusalem, which cometh down out of heaven from my God.

13 He that hath ears let him hear what the Spirit saith unto the churches.

14 For the messenger to the church of Laodicea write; These things saith the faithful and true Witness, who is the origin of the creation of God;

15 I know thy works, that thou art neither cold nor hot:

16 So then because thou art lukewarm, I will spew thee out of my mouth; for thou makest me sick:

17 Because thou sayest, I am rich, and increased with goods, and have need of nothing; and knowest not that thou art wretched, and miserable, and blind, and poor, and naked:

18 I counsel thee to buy for thyself of me gold tried in the fire, that thou mayest be rich, and to put on my white raiment, that the shame of thy nakedness may not appear. And anoint thine eyes with eyesalve, that thou mayest see.

10 As many as I love, I rebuke and chasten: be zealous therefore, and repent.

20 Behold, I stand at the door, and knock: if any man hear my voice, and open the door, I will come in to him, and will sup with him, and he with me.

21 To him that overcometh will I grant to sit with me on my throne.

22 He that hath ears to hear, let him hear what the Spirit saith unto the churches.

BOOK THE THIRD

1 And the first voice which I heard *was* as it were of a trumpet talking with me; which said, Come up hither, and I will shew thee things which must be hereafter.

2 And I was in the Spirit: and, behold, a throne was set in heaven, and one sat on the throne.

3 And he that sat was to look upon like a jasper and a sardine stone: and *there was* a rainbow round about the throne, in sight like unto an emerald.

4 And round about the throne I saw four and twenty seats: and upon the seats four and twenty elders sitting in white raiment, and on their heads crowns of gold.

5 And out of the throne proceed lightnings and voices and thunderings and burning torches of fire, which are spirits.

6 And before the throne, as it were a sea of glass like unto crystal, are the angels of God.

The Story of the Four Living Ones

And I saw in the midst of the throne and round about the throne, four Living Ones, full of eyes before and behind.

7 The first Living One *was* like a lion, and the second Living One like a calf, and the third Living One had a face as a man, and the remaining Living One *was* like a flying eagle.

8 These four Living Ones had each of them six wings about *him;* and they are full of eyes within.

9 And when those Living Ones gave glory to him that sat on the throne,

10 All the elders fell down and worshipped the Lord, and cast their crowns at his feet, and cried, saying,

11 Thou art worthy, O Lord, our God, to receive glory and power: for thou hast created all things, and for thy sake they are and were created.

1 And I saw in the right hand of him that sat on the throne a book, written within and without, and sealed with seven seals.

2 And I heard a strong angel proclaiming with a loud voice, Who is worthy to take the book, and to loose the seals thereof?

3 For no man in heaven, nor in earth, neither under the earth, had been able to open the book, neither to look thereon.

4 And I wept much, because no man was worthy to open the book, neither to look thereon.

5 And one of the elders saith unto me, Behold, the

5. 5-14

Lion of the tribe of Juda, the Root of David, hath conquered that he might open the book, and loose the seals thereof.

6 And I beheld in the midst of the four Living Ones, and in the midst of the elders, a Lamb standing, as it had been slain, having seven horns and seven eyes, which are the spirits of God sent forth into all the earth.

7 And he came and took it out of the right hand of him that sat upon the throne.

8 And when he had taken the book, the four Living Ones and the four *and* twenty elders fell down before the Lamb, having every one of them harps, and golden vials full of odours, which are the prayers of saints.

9 And they were singing a new song, saying, Thou art worthy, O Lord, to take the book, and to open the seals thereof: for thou wast slain, and hast redeemed, O God, in thy blood out of every kindred, and people, and nation, and tongue.

11 And I beheld, and I heard the voice of many angels round about the throne, and round about the Living Ones, and round about the elders. And the number of the angels was ten thousand times ten thousand, and thousands of thousands;

12 Saying with a loud voice, Worthy is the Lamb that was slain to receive power, and godhead, and wisdom, and strength, and honour, and blessing.

13 And every creature which is in heaven, and on the earth, and in the sea, heard I saying, Blessing, and honour, and glory, and power, *be* for ever and ever unto our God.

14 And the four Living Ones and the elders fell down and worshipped God, saying, Amen.

BOOK THE FOURTH

The Story of the Seven Seals

1 And I saw when the Lamb opened one of the seven seals, and I heard one of the four Living Ones saying, like the noise of thunder, Come and see.

2 And behold a white horse: and he that sat on him had a bow; and a crown was given unto him: and the conqueror went forth to conquer.

3 And when he had opened the second seal, I heard the second Living One say, Come and see.

4 And there went out another horse *that was* red: and *power* was given to him that sat thereon to take peace from the earth, and that they should kill one another: and there was given unto him a great sword.

5 And when he had opened the third seal, I heard the third Living One say, Come and see. And lo, a black ox; and he that sat on him had a pair of balances in his hand.

6 And I heard a voice from the midst of the four Living Ones, which said, A measure of wheat for a penny; and *see* thou hurt not the oil and the wine.

7 And when he had opened the fourth seal, I heard the fourth Living One say, Come and see.

8 And behold a pale horse: and his name that sat on him was Death, and Hades followed him. And power was given unto him over the fourth part of the earth, to kill with sword, and with hunger, and with death, and with the beasts of the earth.

The Story of the Souls of the Slain

9 And when he had opened the fifth seal, I saw under the altar of God the souls of them that were slain for the Word of God, and for the testimony unto him which they held:

10 And they cried with a loud voice, saying, How long, O holy Lord, holy and true, dost thou not judge and avenge our blood on them that dwell on the earth?

11 And white robes were given unto every one of them; and it was decreed that they should rest yet for a little season, until the number of their fellow servants, that should be killed as they *were*, should be completed.

The Story of the Sixth Seal

12 And I beheld when he had opened the sixth seal, and there was a great earthquake; and the sun became black as sackcloth, and the whole moon became *as* blood;

13 And the stars fell unto the earth, even as a fig tree loseth its untimely figs, when it is shaken by a mighty wind.

14 And the heaven departed as a scroll when it is rolled together; and every mountain and island were moved out of their places.

15 And the kings of the earth, and the great men, and the chief captains, and the mighty men, and every bond man, and every free man, hid themselves in caves and in the rocks of the mountains;

16 And they said to the rocks and mountains, Fall on us, and hide us from the face of him that sitteth on the throne, and from the wrath of the Lamb:

17 For the great day of their wrath is come; and who can endure it?

The Story of the Four Angels of the Winds

1 And after these things I saw four angels standing on the four corners of the earth, holding the four winds of the earth, that they should not blow on the earth, nor on the sea, nor on any tree.

7. 2-11

2 And I saw another angel ascending from the east, having the seal of the living God: and he cried with a loud voice to the four angels, to whom power was given to hurt the earth and the sea,

3 Saying, Hurt not the earth, neither the sea, nor the trees, till we seal the servants of our God in their foreheads.

The Story of the Hundred and Forty Four Thousand

4 And I heard the number of them which were sealed: *and there were* sealed a hundred *and* forty *and* four thousand of all the tribes of the children of Israel.

5 Of the tribe of Juda *were* sealed twelve thousand. Of the tribe of Reuben *were* sealed twelve thousand. Of the tribe of Gad *were* sealed twelve thousand.

6 Of the tribe of Aser *were* sealed twelve thousand. Of the tribe of Nephthalim *were* sealed twelve thousand. Of the tribe of Manasses *were* sealed twelve thousand.

7 Of the tribe of Simeon *were* sealed twelve thousand. Of the tribe of Issachar *were* sealed twelve thousand. Of the tribe of Levi *were* sealed twelve thousand.

8 Of the tribe of Zabulon *were* sealed twelve thousand. Of the tribe of Joseph *were* sealed twelve thousand. Of the tribe of Benjamin *were* sealed twelve thousand.

9 After this I beheld, and, lo, a great multitude, which no man could number, from all nations, and kindreds, and peoples, and tongues, stood before the throne and before the Lamb, clothed wtih white robes, and palms in their hands;

10 And cried with a loud voice, saying, Salvation belongeth to our God which sitteth upon the throne.

11 And all the angels stood round about the throne, and *about* the elders and the four Living Ones, and fell

before the Lamb on their faces, and worshipped the Lord,

12 Saying, Amen: Blessing, and glory, and wisdom, and thanksgiving, and honour, and power, and might, *be* unto our God for ever and ever. Amen.

13 And one of the elders answered, saying unto me, Who are these which are arrayed in white robes? And whence came they?

14 And I said unto him, Thou knowest, Sir. These are they which come out of much tribulation, and have washed their robes, and made them white in the blood of the Lamb.

15 Therefore are they before the throne of God and serve him day and night on his throne. For he that sitteth on the throne shall dwell among them.

16 And *his* church shall hunger no more, neither thirst any more; neither doth the sun light on them by day, nor the moon by night.

17 For the Lamb which sitteth in the midst of the throne shall be their Shepherd, and shall lead them unto fountains of living water, and wipe away every tear from their eyes.

Explanation of the Seventh Seal

1 And when he had opened the seventh seal, there was a silence in heaven.

BOOK THE FIFTH

2 And I saw seven angels, which stood before God, and had received seven trumpets.

3 And another angel came and stood upon the altar, having a golden censer. And there was given unto him the incense of the prayers of all saints *as he stood* upon the golden altar which is before God.

4 And the smoke of the incense of the prayers of the saints ascended up before God out of the angel's hand.

5 And the angel took the censer, and filled it with fire of the altar, and cast it into the earth: and there were voices, and thunderings, and lightnings, and an earthquake.

6 And the seven angels which had the seven trumpets prepared themselves to sound.

7 The first angel sounded, and there followed hail and fire mingled with blood, and they were cast upon the earth: and the third part of the earth was burnt up, and the third part of trees was burnt up, and all green grass was burnt up.

8 And the second angel sounded, and as it were a great mountain of fire was cast burning into the sea:

9 And the third part of the sea became blood, and the third part of the creatures which were in the sea, and had life, died; and the third part of the ships were destroyed.

10 And the third angel sounded, and a great star fell from heaven, as it were a lamp, and it fell upon the third part of the rivers, and upon the fountains of water;

11 And the name of this star is called Wormwood. And many men died of the waters, because they were made bitter.

12 And the fourth angel sounded, and the third part of the sun was smitten, and the third part of the stars, and the third part of the moon, that the third part of them might be darkened, and *the part* of the day and of the night appear.

13 And I beheld, and heard an angel flying through the midst of heaven, saying with a loud voice, Woe, woe, woe, to the dwellers on the earth by reason of

the voices of the trumpet of the three angels, which are yet to sound!

1 And the fifth angel sounded, and a star fell from heaven unto the earth. And to him was given the key of the abyss.

2 And there arose a smoke out of the abyss, as the smoke of a great furnace; and the sun and the air were darkened by reason of the smoke.

3 And there came out of the smoke locusts upon the earth: and unto them was given power, as the scorpions of the earth have power.

4 And it was commanded them that they should not hurt the grass of the earth, neither any green thing; but only those men which have not the seal of God in their forehead.

5 And to them it was given that they should not kill them, but that they should torment them five months: and their torment *was* as the torment of a scorpion, when it stingeth a man.

6 And men shall seek death, and shall not find it; and shall desire to die, and death shall flee from them.

The Story of the Locusts

7 And the shapes of the locusts *were* like unto horses prepared unto battle; and on their heads were crowns like gold, and their faces *were* as the faces of men.

8 And they had hair as the hair of women, and their teeth were as *the teeth* of lions.

9 And they had bodies as it were breastplates of iron; and the sound of their wings *was* as the sound of many chariots rushing to battle.

10 And they had tails like unto scorpions, and there were stings in their tails: and their power *was* to hurt men five months.

9. 11-20

11 And they have as king over them the angel of the abyss. His name in the Hebrew tongue is Abaddon, in the Greek tongue Apollyon, and in the Latin tongue Destroyer.

12 One woe is past; *and*, behold, there come two woes more hereafter.

The Story of the Sixth Trumpet

13 And the sixth angel sounded, and I heard an angel from the four horns of the golden altar which is before God,

14 Saying to the sixth angel, which had the trumpet, Loose the four angels which are bound in the great river Euphrates.

15 And the four angels were loosed that they might prepare to slay the third part of men.

16 And the number of the horses *were* thousands of thousands.

The Story of the Horses

17 I saw the horses in the vision, and them that sat on them. They had breastplates of fire, and of jacinth, and brimstone: and the heads of the horses were as *the heads* of lions; and out of their mouths issued fire and smoke and brimstone.

18 By these three plagues was the third part of men killed, by the fire, and by the smoke, and by the brimstone, which issued out of their mouths.

19 The power of the horses is in their mouths, and in their tails: for their tails *were* like unto serpents, and had heads, and with them they do hurt.

20 And the rest of the men which were not killed by these plagues repented not of their former works, that they should not worship devils, and idols of silver, and gold, and brass, and iron, and stone, and of wood; which neither can walk nor see.

21 Neither repented they of their murders, nor of their fornication, nor of their thefts.

The Story of the Mighty Angel

1 And I saw another mighty angel come down from heaven, clothed with a cloud: and a rainbow *was* upon his head, and his face *was* as it were the sun, and his feet as pillars of fire:

2 And he had in his hand an open book: and he set his right foot upon the sea, and *his* left *foot* on the earth,

3 And cried with a loud voice, as *when* a lion roareth: and when he had cried, seven thunders uttered their voices.

4 And the things which the seven thunders had uttered, I was about to write. And I heard a voice from heaven saying, Seal up those things which the seven thunders uttered, and write them not.

5 And the angel which I saw stand upon the sea and upon the earth lifted up his right hand to heaven,

6 And sware by him that liveth for ever and ever, who created ~~the heaven by~~ his word, and the earth, and the things that therein are, and the sea, and the things which are therein, that there should be time no longer:

7 But in the days of the voice of the seventh angel, when he shall begin to sound, and the mystery of God hath been fulfilled as he promised by his prophets.

8 And I heard a voice from heaven of an angel of God speaking unto me, and saying, Go *and* take the book which is open in the hand of the angel which standeth upon the sea and upon the earth.

9 And I went unto the angel, and said, Give me the book. And he said unto me, Take *it*, and eat it up;

10. 9—11. 7

and it shall make thy belly bitter, but it shall be in thy mouth sweet as honey.

10 And I took the book out of the angel's hand, and ate it up; and it was in my mouth as sweet honey: and as soon as I had eaten it, my belly was filled with bitterness.

11 And he said unto me, Thou must preach the advent of the Lord, before peoples, and tongues, and nations, and many kings.

1 And there was given me a reed like unto a rod: and the angel stood, saying unto me, Rise, and measure the temple of God, and the altar, and them that worship therein.

2 But the court which is without the temple leave out, and measure it not; for it is given unto the Gentiles to trample under foot the holy city, and they shall trample *it* under foot forty *and* two months.

The Story of Elias and Enoch

3 And I will speak unto my two witnesses, and they shall prophesy a thousand two hundred *and* ninety days, clothed in sackcloth.

4 These are the two olive trees, and the two candlesticks standing before the Lord of the earth.

5 And if any man desire to hurt them, fire shall proceed out of their mouth, and devour their enemies: and if any man desire to hurt them, he must in this manner be killed.

6 These have power to shut heaven, that it rain not in the days of their prophecy: and have power over waters to turn them to blood, and to smite the earth with all plagues, as often as they will.

7 False testimony shall overcome them, and kill them.

11. 7-15

8 And the bodies of the witnesses shall be cast out into the street of a great city.

9 And they of the people and kindreds and tongues and nations shall see their dead bodies three days and a half, and shall not suffer their dead bodies to be put in graves.

10 And they that dwell upon the earth shall rejoice over them, and make merry, and shall send gifts one to another; because these two prophets tormented them that dwelt on the earth.

The Story of the Same Witnesses

11 And after three days and a half the Spirit of life from God entered into them, and they stood upon their feet; and great fear fell upon them which saw them.

12 And I heard a great voice, which said, Come up hither. And they ascended up to heaven in a cloud; and their enemies beheld them.

13 And the same hour was there a great earthquake, and the tenth part of the city fell, and in the earthquake were slain of men seven thousand: and the remnant were affrighted, and gave glory to the God of heaven.

14 The second woe is past; that which follows is the third woe.

The Seventh Trumpet, or the Resurrection of All Flesh

15 And the seventh angel sounded; and there were great voices in heaven, The kingdom of our Lord Jesus Christ is come; and he shall reign for ever and ever. Amen.

11. 19—12. 9
BOOK THE SIXTH

19 And the temple of God was opened in heaven, and there was seen in his temple the ark of the testament: and there were lightnings, and voices, and thunderings, and an earth quake, and great hail. And I saw the beast ascend from the abyss.

Concerning the Woman and the Beast

1 And there appeared a great wonder in heaven; a woman with the sun and the moon under her feet, and upon her head a crown of twelve stars:

3 And there appeared another wonder, even a great red dragon, having seven heads and ten horns, and upon his heads seven crowns.

4 And his tail drew the third part of the stars of heaven, and did cast them to the earth. And the dragon stood before the woman which was ready to be delivered, to kill her child as soon as it was born.

5 And the woman brought forth a man child, who was to rule all nations with a rod of iron: and her child was caught up unto God, and to his throne.

6 And the woman fled into the wilderness, where she hath a place prepared by God, that they should feed her there a thousand two hundred *and* ninety days.

7 And there was war in heaven: Michael and his angels fought against the dragon; and the dragon fought and his angels,

8 And prevailed not; neither was their place found any more in heaven.

9 And the great dragon was cast out, the old serpent, called the Devil, and Satan, which deceiveth the whole world: he was cast out into the earth, and his angels were cast out with him.

10 And I heard a loud voice saying in heaven, Now is come the salvation of our God, Jesus Christ; for the accuser of our brethren hath been confounded, who accuses us day and night.

11 And they overcame him in the blood of the Lamb. And for the word of their testimony they loved not their lives, that now they might be in heaven.

12 Woe to you, earth and sea! for the devil is come down unto you, having great wrath, because he knoweth that he hath but a short time.

13 And when the dragon saw that he was confined to the earth, he persecuted the woman which brought forth the man *child*.

14 And to the woman were given two wings of the great eagle that she might fly into the wilderness, into her place, and be nourished there for a time, times, and half a time, from the face of the serpent.

15 And the serpent cast out of his mouth water as a flood after the woman, that he might carry her away with the flood.

16 And the earth helped the woman; and the earth opened her mouth, and swallowed up the flood which the dragon cast out of his mouth.

17 And the dragon was wroth with the woman, and went to make war with the remnant of her seed, as long as they keep the commandments of God, and have the testimony of Jesus Christ. And he stood on the sand of the sea shore.

The Story of the Beast and This Same Dragon

1 And I saw a beast rise up out of the sea, having ten horns and seven heads; and his horns *were* ten crowns, and upon his heads *were* names of blasphemy.

2 And the beast which I saw was like unto a leopard, and his feet were as *the feet* of a bear, and his mouth

13. 2-12

as *the mouth* of a lion. And the dragon gave unto him his power.

3 And I saw one of the heads as it were wounded to death; and his deadly wound was healed: and all the world wondered and followed after the beast.

4 And they worshipped the dragon because he gave power unto the beast; and they worshipped the beast, saying, Who *is* like unto the beast? who is able to make war with him?

5 And there was given unto him a mouth speaking great blasphemies; and the power was given unto him to continue forty *and* two months.

6 At the last he opened his mouth in blasphemy against God, to blaspheme his name, and his tabernacle, and them that dwell in heaven.

7 And it was given unto him to make war with the saints, and to overcome them: and power was given him over all kindreds, and peoples, and tongues, and nations.

8 And all that dwell upon the earth shall worship him; for his name was not written in the book of life of the Lamb from the foundation of the world.

9 He that hath ears, let him hear.

10 If any man goeth into captivity, he that killeth him with the sword killeth him with the sword as a captive. Here is seduction, and the virtue of the saints.

The Story of the Third Beast

11 And I beheld another beast coming up out of the earth. He had two horns like a lamb, and he shewed himself as a lamb with his own, and put on the appearance of a righteous man, and spake as a dragon.

12 And he exercised all the power of the first beast in his sight, and causeth the earth and them which

dwell therein to worship the first beast, whose deadly wound was healed.

13 And he doeth great wonders, so that he even maketh fire come down from heaven on the earth in the sight of men,

14 And deceiveth them that dwell on the earth by *means* of those miracles which have been given him to do, even to making an image of the beast, as though it had been wounded *to death* by a sword, and did live.

15 And it was given him to give life unto the image of the beast, And he will cause as many as do not worship the image of the beast to be killed.

16 And he maketh all, both small and great, rich and poor, free and bond, to receive a mark in their right hand, or in their foreheads.

The Story of the Sealed

1 And I looked, and lo, a Lamb stood on the mount Sion, and with him a hundred forty *and* four thousand, having his name and his Father's written in their foreheads.

2 And I heard a voice as the voice of many waters, and as the voice of a great thunder. And the voice I heard was as the voice of harpers harping with their harps:

3 And they sing as it were a new song before the thorne, and before the *four* Living Ones, and before the elders: and no man can sing the song but the hundred *and* forty *and* four thousand, which were redeemed from the earth.

4 These are they which are not joined unto wives; for they are virgins. These follow the Lamb whithersoever he goeth. These were redeemed from the beginning unto God and to the Lamb.

5 And in their mouth is found no guile.

14. 6-15

BOOK THE SEVENTH

6 And I saw another angel fly in the midst of heaven, having the everlasting gospel to preach unto them that dwell on the earth, and to every nation, and kindred, and tongue, and people,

7 Saying, Fear the Lord, and give glory to him; for the hour of his judgment is come: and worship him that made heaven, and earth, the sea, and the fountains of waters.

8 And a second angel followed, saying, Babylon the mighty is fallen, is fallen, because she made all nations drink of the wine of her fornication.

9 And a third angel followed them, saying with a loud voice, If any man worship the beast and his image, and receive *his* mark in his forehead,

10 The same shall drink of the wine of the wrath of God, and shall be tormented with fire and brimstone in the presence of the holy angels, and in the presence of the Lamb:

11 And the smoke from their torments ascendeth up for ever and ever: and they have no rest day or night, who worship the beast and his image, and whosoever receiveth the mark of his name.

12 This is the patience of the saints, to keep the commandments of God, and the faith of Jesus.

13 And I heard a voice from heaven saying, Write, Blessed *are* the dead which die in Christ.

The Story of the White Cloud

14 And I looked, and behold a white cloud, and upon the cloud *one* like unto the Son of man, having on his head a golden crown, and in his hand he had a sharp sickle.

15 And an angel came out of the temple, crying with

14. 15-15. 4

a loud voice to him that sat on the cloud, Thrust in thy sickle, and reap: for the time is come to reap; for the harvest of the earth is ripe.

16 And he that sat on the cloud thrust in his sickle on the earth; and the earth was reaped.

17 And another angel came out of the temple which is in heaven, he also having a sharp sickle.

18 And another angel *came out* from the altar, which had power over fire; and cried with a loud cry to him that had a sharp sickle, saying, Thrust in thy sharp sickle, and gather the clusters of the vineyard of the earth; for her grapes are fully ripe.

19 And the angel thrust in his sickle into the earth, and gathered the vineyard of the earth, and cast *it* into the great winepress.

20 And the winepress was trodden without the city, and blood came out of the winepress, even unto the horses' bridles, by the space of a thousand *and* six hundred furlongs.

The Story of the Seven Angels

1 And I saw another sign in heaven, great and marvellous, seven angels having the seven last plagues; for in them is fulfilled the wrath of God.

2 And I saw as it were a sea of glass mingled with fire, and the Conqueror of the beast, and of his image. And *I saw* the number *of those* of his name, standing on the sea of glass, and having the harps of God,

3 And singing the song of Moses the servant of God. And they were singing unto the Lamb, Great and marvellous *are* thy works, O God Almighty; just and true *are* thy ways, thou King of the nations.

4 Who should not fear thee, O Lord, and glorify thy name? for *thou* only *art* holy: for all nations shall come and worship before thee; for thy righteousness is made manifest.

15. 5—16. 6

The Story of the Open Temple and of the Vials

5 And after that I looked, and, behold, the temple of the tabernacle of the testimony in heaven was opened:

6 And the seven angels, which have the seven plagues, came out of the temple, clothed in pure and white linen, and having their breasts girded with golden girdles.

7 And one of the four Living Ones gave unto the seven angels seven golden vials full of the wrath of God, who liveth for ever and ever.

8 And the temple was filled with smoke from the glory of God, and from his power; and no man was able to enter the temple, till the seven plagues of the seven angels were fulfilled.

BOOK THE EIGHTH

1 And I heard a great voice saying to the seven angels, Go your ways, and pour out the vials of the wrath of God upon the earth.

2 And the first angel went, and poured out his vial upon the earth; and there fell a noisome and grievous sore upon the men which had the name of the beast, and *upon* them which worshipped his image.

3 And the second angel went and poured out his vial upon the sea; and it became as the blood of a dead *man:* and every living soul died in the sea.

4 And the third angel poured out his vial upon the rivers and fountains of waters; and they became blood.

5 And I heard a voice from the waters say, Thou art righteous, O Thou, which wast, and shalt be holy, because thou hast judged thus.

6 And because they shed blood, the blood of Christ

16. 6-17

and of the prophets, thou hast given them blood to drink; for they are worthy.

7 And I heard the altar of God say, Yea, the Lord God Almighty; true and righteous are his judgments.

8 And the fourth angel poured out his vial upon the sun; and it was given unto him to scorch *men* with fire.

9 And men were scorched with great heat, and blasphemed the name of God, which hath power over these plagues: and they repented not to give him glory.

10 And the fifth angel poured out his vial upon the beast; and his kingdom was made full of darkness; and they gnawed their tongues for pain,

11 And blasphemed because of the wrath of God, and repented not.

12 And the sixth angel poured out his vial upon the great Euphrates; and the water thereof was dried up, that the way of those kings which are from the east might be prepared.

The Story of the Frogs

13 And I saw unclean spirits like frogs *come* out of the mouth of the dragon, and out of the mouth of the beast, and out of the mouth of the false prophet.

14 For the frogs are the spirits of devils, working miracles, which go forth unto the kings of the whole world, to gather them to the battle of the great day of the Lord Almighty.

15 Behold he cometh as a thief. Blessed *is* he that watcheth, and keepeth his garments, lest he walk naked, and they see his shame.

16 And he gathered them together into a place called in the Hebrew tongue Armageddon.

17 And the seventh angel poured out his vial into the air; and there came a great voice from the throne, saying, It is done.

16. 18—17. 5

18 And there were lightnings, and voices, and thunders; and there was a great earthquake.
19 And the great city was divided into three parts, and he poured out upon her the cup of the wine of his wrath.
20 And every island fled away, and the mountains were not found.
21 And there was a great hail, *every stone* about the weight of a talent, which fell upon all men from heaven; and men openly blasphemed the God Christ because of the plague of the hail; for the plague thereof was exceeding great.

BOOK THE NINTH

1 And there came one of the seven angels which had the vials, and talked with me, saying, Come, *and* I will shew unto thee the judgment of the great harlot that sitteth upon the many hills;
2 With whom the kings of the earth have committed fornication, and the inhabitants of the earth have been made drunk with the wine of her fornication.
3 So he carried me away in the spirit into the wilderness.

The Story of This Woman and of the Beast

And I saw a woman sit upon a scarlet coloured beast, full of all blasphemies, having seven heads and ten horns.
4 And the woman was arrayed in purple and saffron, and decked with gold and precious stones and pearls, having a golden cup in her hand full of abominations, and of the filthiness of her fornication:
5 And upon her forehead *was* a name written, Mystery, Babylon the Great, the Mother of the Harlots of the Earth.

6 And I saw the woman drunken with the blood of the saints, and with the blood of the martyrs of Jesus: and when I saw *it*, I wondered with great admiration.

7 And the angel said unto me, Wherefore didst thou marvel? I will tell thee the mystery of the woman, and of the beast that carrieth her, which hath the seven heads and ten horns.

8 This is the beast that thou sawest; he was, and is not. And they that dwell on the earth wondered, when they beheld the beast; for he was, and is not, and is born.

9 Here *is* the meaning to him which hath wisdom. The seven heads are seven mountains, on which the woman sitteth.

10 And there are seven kings: five are fallen, and one is, *and* the other is not yet come; and when he cometh, he must continue a short space.

11 And the beast that was, and is not, even he is the eighth, and is of the seven, and goeth into perdition.

12 And the ten horns which thou sawest are ten kings, which have received no kingdom as yet; but receive power as kings one hour after the beast.

13 These have *all* one mind, and give their power and strength unto the beast.

The Lamb and the Conquering of the Beast

14 These ten kings make war with the Lamb, and the Lamb shall overcome them: for he is Lord of lords, and King of kings: and they that are with him *are* called, and chosen, and faithful.

15 And he saith, This beast which thou beholdest, on which the harlot sitteth, are peoples, and multitudes, and nations, and tongues.

16 And the ten horns which thou sawest, these hate

17. 16—18. 7

the harlot, and shall make her desolate and naked, and shall eat her flesh, and burn her with fire.

17 For God put *it* into their hearts to fulfill his decree, and give their kingdom unto the beast, until *such time as* the words of God should be fulfilled.

18 And the woman which thou sawest is that great city, which reigneth over the kings of the earth.

BOOK THE TENTH

The Story of the City of the Devil

1 After these things I saw another angel come down from heaven, having great power; and the earth was lightened with his glory.

2 And he cried mightily, saying, Babylon the great is fallen, is fallen, and is become the habitation of devils, and the hold of every unclean bird, and foul spirit.

3 For all nations have drunk of the wine of her fornication, and the kings of the earth have committed fornication with her, and the merchants of the earth are waxed rich through the might of her glory.

4 And I heard another voice, saying, Come out of her, my people, and be not partakers of her sins, nor hurt by her plagues.

5 For her sins have reached unto heaven, and God hath remembered her iniquities.

6 Reward her even as she rewarded others, and double unto her double according to her works: in the cup which she hath filled, fill to her double.

7 How much she hath glorified herself, so much torment and sorrow give her: for she saith in her heart, I sit a queen, and am no widow, and shall see no sorrow.

8 Therefore shall her plagues come in one day, death, and mourning, and fire; for strong *is* the Lord God who shall judge her.

9 And the kings of the earth, who have committed fornication with her, shall bewail her, when they shall see the smoke.

10 Standing afar off for fear of her, saying, Alas, alas, thou great city Babylon, thou mighty city! for in one hour is thy condemnation come.

11 And the merchants of the earth shall mourn over her; for no man buyeth their merchandise any more:

12 This merchandise of gold, and of silver, and of iron,

13 And of cinnamon, and all ointments, and wheat, and horses, and cattle:

14 *All* are departed from thee, and thou shalt find them no more.

15 And the merchants of these things, who were made rich by her, shall stand afar off,

16 Saying, Alas, alas, that great city, which was clothed in fine linen, and purple, and scarlet, and decked with gold, and precious stones, and pearls!

17 For in one hour so great riches is come to nought. And every shipmaster, and all the company in ships, and sailors, and as many as trade by sea, stood afar off,

19 And cried, weeping and wailing, Alas, alas, that great city, wherein were made rich all that had ships in the sea by reason of her wealth! for in one hour is she made desolate.

20 Heaven rejoices over her, and apostles and prophets; for God hath pronounced judgment upon her.

The Story of the Mighty Angel

21 And a mighty angel took up a stone like a great

18. 21—19. 8

millstone, and cast *it* into the sea, saying, Thus with violence shall that great city Babylon be thrown down, and shall be no more at all.

22 And the voice of harpers, and of musicians, and pipers, and trumpeters, shall be heard no more at all in her;

23 For her merchants were great men of the earth; for by her sorceries were all nations deceived.

24 And in her was found the blood of prophets, and of saints.

The Story of the City of God

1 After these things I heard a voice as of great multitudes in heaven, saying, Alleluia; Salvation, and glory, and honour, and power, belong unto our God:

2 For both true and righteous are *his* judgments; for he hath judged the great harlot, which did corrupt the earth with her fornication, and hath avenged the blood of his servants at her hand.

3 And again they said, Alleluia. And the smoke rose up for ever and ever.

4 And the four and twenty elders and the four Living Ones fell down and worshipped God that sat on the throne, saying, Amen; and Alleluia.

5 And a voice came out of the throne, saying, Praise our God, ye his servants, and ye that fear him, both small and great.

6 And I heard as it were the voice of a trumpet, and as the voice of many waters, and as the voice of mighty thunderings, saying, Alleluia: for our Lord God reigneth omnipotent.

7 Let us be glad and rejoice, and glorify his name: for the marriage of the Lamb is come, and his wife hath made herself ready.

8 And to her it hath been granted that she should be

19. 8-17

arrayed in his shining and white raiment; for his raiment is the righteousness of the saints.

9 And the angel said, Write, These are the true sayings of God.

10 And I fell at his feet to worship him. And the angel said, See thou do *it* not: I am thy fellow servant, and one of thy brethren that have the testimony of Christ Jesus: worship the Lord. The testimony of Christ Jesus is the spirit of prophecy.

[*The Story of the White Horse and the Word of God*]

11 And I saw heaven opened, and behold a white horse; and he that sat upon him *was* called Faithful and True, and in righteousness he doth judge and make war.

12 His eyes *were* as a flame of fire, and *there were* crowns on his head; and he had a name written, that no man knew but himself.

13 And he *was* clothed in a garment sprinkled with blood: and his name was called The Word of God.

14 And the armies *which were* in heaven followed upon white horses, clothed in raiment white and clean.

15 And out of his mouth went a sharp sword, that with it he should smite the nations; and he ruleth them with a rod of iron: and he treadeth the winepress of the wrath of Almighty God.

16 And he hath on *his* vesture over his thigh a name written, King of kings, and Lord of lords.

The Story of the Angel Standing in the Sun

17 And I saw an angel standing in the sun; and he cried with a loud voice, saying to all the birds that fly in the midst of heaven, Come *and* gather yourselves together unto the supper of God;

19. 18—20. 4

18 That ye may eat the flesh of kings, and the flesh of captains, and the flesh of mighty men, and the flesh of all *men, both* free and bond, both small and great.

The Story of the Beast and the Kings of the Earth

19 And I saw the beast, and the kings of the earth, and their armies, gathered together to make war against him that sat on the white horse, and against his army.

20 And the beast was taken, and with him the false prophet and those that wrought miracles before him, with which he deceived them that had received the mark of the beast, and them that worshipped his image.

21 And the remnant were slain with the sword of him that sat upon the horse, which *sword* proceeded out of his mouth. And all the birds were filled with their flesh.

The Story of the Other Angel

1 And I saw an angel come down from heaven, having the key of the abyss, and a great chain in his hand.

2 And he laid hold on the dragon, the old serpent, which is the devil, and Satan, and bound him a thousand years.

3 And the angel cast him into the abyss, and set a seal upon him, till the thousand years should be fulfilled. And after that he must be loosed a little season.

Concerning the Souls of the Slain

4 And I saw thrones, and those that sat upon them, and judgment was given unto them. And I saw the

20. 4-12

souls of them that were slain for the witness of Jesus, and for the word of God. And as many as had not worshipped the beast, neither his image, neither had received his mark upon their forehead, nor in their hand, lived and reigned with Christ a thousand years.

6 Blessed and holy *is* he that hath part in the first resurrection: on such death shall have no power, but they shall be priests of God and of Christ, and the Holy Spirit shall dwell with them.

The Loosing of the Devil

7 And when the thousand years are expired, Satan shall be loosed out of his prison,

8 And shall go out to deceive the nations which are in the four quarters of the earth, Gog and Magog: the number of whom is as the sand of the sea.

9 And they went up on the high places of the earth, and compassed the camp of the saints about, and the beloved city.

Of the Devil, the Beast, and the False Prophet

And fire came down from God out of heaven, and devoured his enemies.

10 And the devil that deceived them was cast into the lake of fire and brimstone, where are the beast and the false prophet.

The Story of the Judgment

11 And I saw a great white throne, and him that sat on it, from whose face the earth and the heaven fled away; and there was found no place for them.

12 And I saw the dead, small and great, stand before the throne, and the books were opened: and an-

other book was opened, *the book* of life: and the dead were judged out of those things which were written in the book, according to their works.

13 And the sea gave up her dead; and death and Hades delivered up their dead.

Of the City of Jerusalem

1 And I saw a new heaven and a new earth. The first heaven had passed away; and there was no more sea.

2 And I saw the holy city, new Jerusalem, gathered together by God *to be* as it were a bride adorned for her husband.

3 And I heard a great voice out of heaven saying, Behold, the tabernacle of God *is* with men; he will dwell with them; and they shall be his people, and God himself shall be with them, *and be* their God.

4 And he shall wipe away every tear from their eyes; and there shall be no more death, and there shall be no more sorrow, neither pain.

5 And he that sat upon the throne said, Behold, I make all things new. And he said, Write: for these words are faithful and true, and I will fulfill them:

6 I am Alpha and Omega, the beginning and the end. I will give unto the faithful water from the fountain of life freely.

7 He that overcometh shall inherit these things; and I will be his God, and he shall be my son.

8 But the faithless, and unbelieving in spirit, and the abominable, and murderers, and sorcerers, and idolaters, and all liars, shall have their part in the lake of the devil, which is the death of the spirit.

9 And he spake with me, saying, Come, and I will shew thee the wife of the Lamb

10 And he led me in the spirit to a high mountain, and shewed me the holy city, Jerusalem.

21. 11—22. 5

11 Her light *was* as that of a stone most precious, as it were of a stone in the likeness of a crystal;

12 And the holy city, Jerusalem, hath over her gates twelve cornices, and names written thereon, which are *the names* of the twelve children of Israel.

13 On the east *she hath* three gates; on the west three gates; on the north three gates; and on the south three gates.

14 And the wall of the city hath twelve foundations, and in them the names of the messengers of the Lamb.

15 And he that talked with me had a golden reed to measure the city, and the gates thereof, and the walls thereof.

16 And the city lieth foursquare, and the length is as large as the breadth: and he measured the city, twelve furlongs. The length and the breadth of it are equal. And the walls of the city *are* pure gold, like unto clear glass.

17 And he measured the walls thereof, four cubits, *according to* the measure of a man, that is, of the angel.

25 And the gates thereof are never shut.

1 And he shewed me a river of water, like crystal, issuing from the throne of the Lamb into the midst of the street thereof.

2 On either side of the river, *was there* the tree of life, yielding its fruit every month: and the leaves of the tree *are* for the healing of the nations:

3 And there shall be no more sickness. The throne of God and of the Lamb shall be therein; and his servants shall serve him:

4 And they shall see his face; and his name *shall be* in their foreheads.

5 And there shall be no more night. And they shall not need candle light and sunlight; for the Lord

22. 5-17

God giveth them light. And the Holy Spirit of love shall dwell with them for ever and ever.

The Last Story of This Book

6 And the angel said, These sayings *are* faithful and true: and the Lord Spirit of the prophets hath sent his angel to shew unto his servants the things which must shortly be done.

7 Blessed *is* he that keepeth the sayings of this book.

8 And when I had heard and seen him I fell down before the feet of the angel which shewed me these things that I might worship him.

9 And he said unto me, I am thy fellow servant, and one of thy brethren which keep the sayings of this book: worship the Lord.

10 And he said unto me, Seal not the sayings of prophecy of this book: for the time is at hand.

11 He that is unjust, let him act unjustly still: and he which is filthy, let him be filthy still.

12 Behold, I come quickly; and my reward *is* with me, to give every man according as his work shall be.

13 I *am* Alpha and Omega, the first and the last, the beginning and the end.

14 Blessed *are* they that keep my commandments, that they may have a right to the tree of life, and enter through the gates into the holy city.

15 Without *are* dogs, and sorcerers, and fornicators, and murderers, and idolaters, and whosoever loveth and maketh a lie.

16 I have sent John *as my* messenger to testify unto you these things in the churches. I am the root and the offspring of David, *and* the bright and morning star.

17 And the Spirit and the bride say, Come. And let him that heareth say, Come. And he that is athirst,

22. 18-21

let him come and drink; for he shall receive the water of life freely.

18 I testify unto every man that heareth the words of prophecy of this book, If any man shall add unto these things, God shall add unto him the plagues written in this book:

19 And if any man shall take away from the words of this prophecy, God shall take away his part from the holy city, and *from* the things which are written in this book.

20 He which testifieth these things saith, Surely I come quickly. Come, Lord Jesus Christ.

21 Thanks be unto God: the grace of our Lord Jesus Christ is with every church. Amen.

TO THE READER

In the above translation I have faithfully translated the old-Latin text of the Spanish MS. throughout, except in four instances [1. 7, 2. 11, 5. 9 and 7. 17], where the reading now found in our MS. has been revised and conformed to the Vulgate. In these four places the unrevised text has been restored from other old-Latin MSS. containing pre-Vulgate readings.

BIBLIOLIFE

Old Books Deserve a New Life
www.bibliolife.com

Did you know that you can get most of our titles in our trademark **EasyScript**™ print format? **EasyScript**™ provides readers with a larger than average typeface, for a reading experience that's easier on the eyes.

Did you know that we have an ever-growing collection of books in many languages?

Order online:
www.bibliolife.com/store

Or to exclusively browse our **EasyScript**™ collection:
www.bibliogrande.com

At BiblioLife, we aim to make knowledge more accessible by making thousands of titles available to you – quickly and affordably.

Contact us:
BiblioLife
PO Box 21206
Charleston, SC 29413